AUTHENTIC TRANSCRIPTIONS
WITH NOTES & TABLATURE

ERIC JOH

GUITAR TRANSCRIPTIONS

ISBN 0-7935-0311-6

FRONT COVER PHOTO: Michael J. Insuaste/IMAGERY
CONCEPT: Mario Contreras

BACK COVER PHOTO: © 1990 Max Crace

HAL•LEONARD™
CORPORATION
7777 W. BLUEMOUND RD. P.O. BOX 13819 MILWAUKEE, WI 53213

AGFA APX 100

AGFA APX 100

C O N T E N T S

Very few post-Hendrix guitarists have conjured 6-string magic as well as Eric Johnson. There's no hint of anger, angst, or sloppiness in any of his playing; instead, each note, each phrase shines like a perfect polished gem. Joyous celebrations, his solos somehow seem to grow more magnificent with each listening.

Even in the dim reaches of his unsigned past, Eric was being lauded by famous players such as Johnny Winter, Billy Gibbons, and Steve Morse; Jeff Baxter went so far as to liken him to "a Jimi Hendrix who had gone on to study with Howard Roberts for eight years!" Despite the accolades, Johnson labored in relative obscurity in Austin, Texas, until the 1986 release of *Tones.* His goal was music that entertains and heals, and his playing was almost beyond belief, marrying deep emotion with mind-boggling technical finesse. The album's collage of guitar sounds ranged from purest-of-pure Strat to Hendrix-approved psychedelia, and won Johnson that year's *Guitar Player Magazine* Readers Poll award for Best New Talent.

Eric spent nearly two years producing his 1990 follow-up, *Ah Via Musicom,* but the wait was worth it. Full of fire and swirling thunder, it's an artistic triumph, as powerful a statement for Eric Johnson as *Electric Ladyland* was for Jimi Hendrix. Johnson's obsessed with tone, and it shows in every facet of his playing.

—Jas Obrecht
Guitar Player Magazine

"Eric Johnson is great. I can't say enough good stuff about him. He's definitely one of the most sophisticated guitarists to come out of Texas."

—Johnny Winter

"Eric Johnson has the most beautiful tone all the way around. It's very, very masculine, and round and warm and dark. Even though he's from Texas, he doesn't have that gunslinger mentality of 'I'm going to kick your butt with my gun.' He is very pure. You can see it in his eyes: 'Okay, I got my tone and my vision, and that's good enough. The Lord will provide the rest.' He has a beautiful soul."

—Carlos Santana

"Eric is a wonderful cat and an honest human being. He has always been one of my favorite people in the world, as well as one of my favorite guitar players. The guy has done more *trying* to be the best that he can be than anybody I've ever seen. Just listen to him and learn."

—Stevie Ray Vaughan

"Eric's extremely expressive. Not only does he have a lot of flash, but he also finesses these amazing, complex lines with very intricate fingerings. He creates great rhythm parts and has fabulous tones."

—Steve Morse

"Eric Johnson? Damn, that guy can play!"

—Billy Gibbons

Bristol Shore

By Eric Johnson

G/F   Fsus2

Intro
 Moderately Fast Rock ♩ = 154

* Notes in parentheses played 2nd time only.

%S Verse

Gtr. 1: w/ Rhy. Fig. 1, 2 times, simile

1. There's	a	place _____		I	dream	of _____			with
2. Nep -	tune	World _____		she	loves	most _____			
3. There's	a	light _____		shin -	ing	near _____			

far	a -	way. _____			
o -	cean	breeze. _____			
off	the	bay. _____			

Gtr. 3: w/ Fill 3, 2nd & 3rd times

There's	a	girl _____		liv -	ing	there _____		and
She	pro -	tects _____		the Tri -	dent	Coast _____		
Through	the	si - ren _____		winds	I	hear _____		

Gtr. 2: w/ Fill 2

by	the	bay. _____	
sev -	en	seas. _____	
that	girl	say. _____	

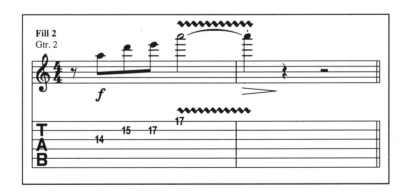

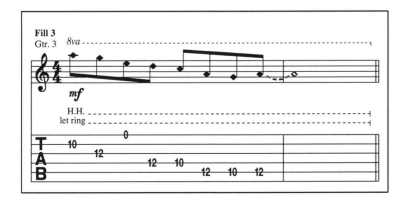

9

Bridge

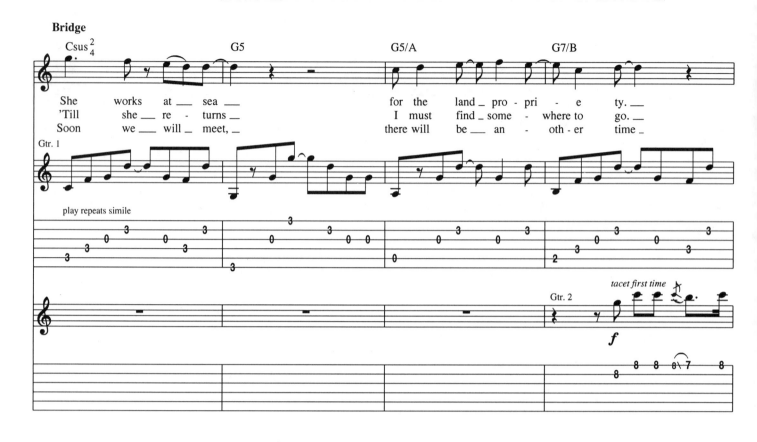

She works at sea ___ for the land ___ pro-pri-e ___ ty. ___
'Till she ___ re-turns ___ I must find ___ some-where to go. ___
Soon we ___ will ___ meet, ___ there will be an-oth-er time ___

Gtr. 1

play repeats simile

tacet first time

Gtr. 2

f

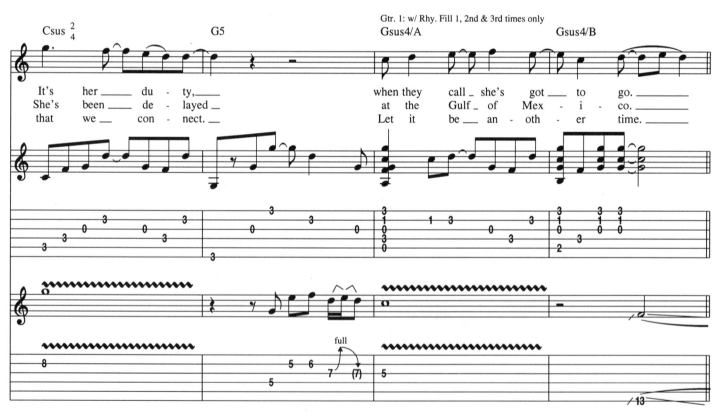

Gtr. 1: w/ Rhy. Fill 1, 2nd & 3rd times only

It's her ___ du ___ ty, ___ when they call ___ she's got ___ to go. ___
She's been ___ de-layed ___ at the Gulf ___ of Mex-i-co. ___
that we ___ con-nect. ___ Let it be an-oth-er time. ___

full

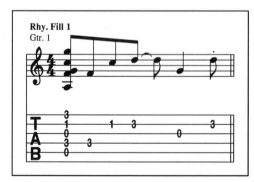

Rhy. Fill 1
Gtr. 1

* Koto style

* Right hand's index finger taps and releases note. Right hand's thumb assists tap by plucking the appropriate string.

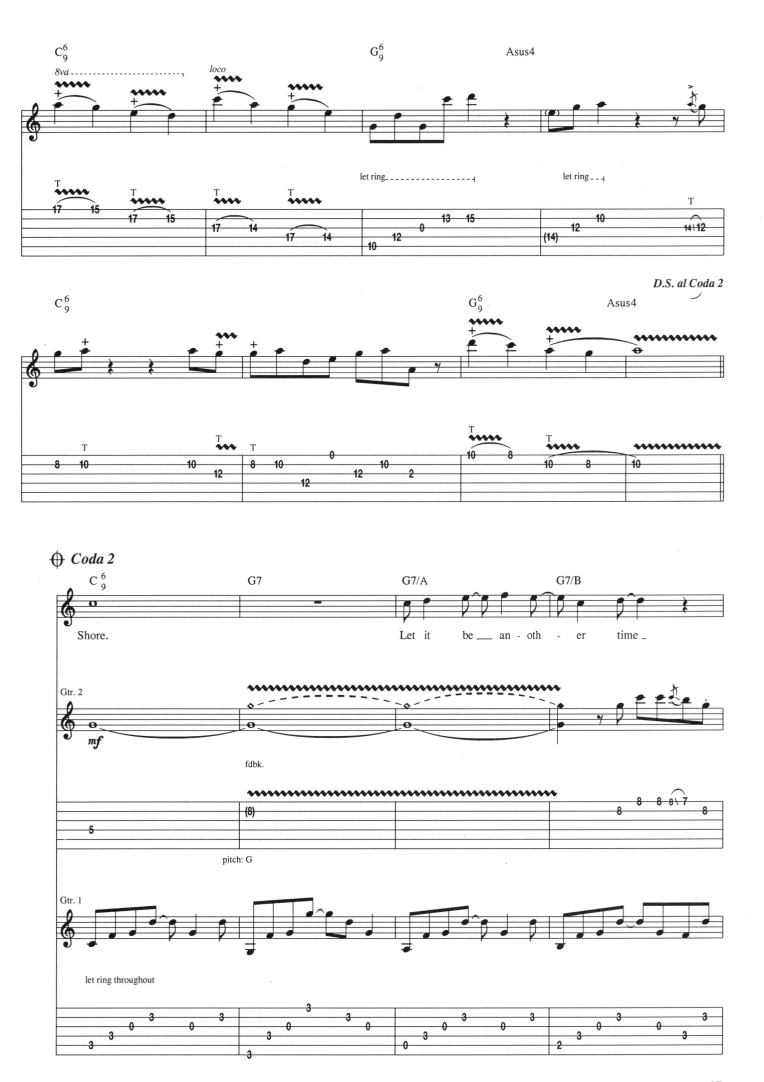

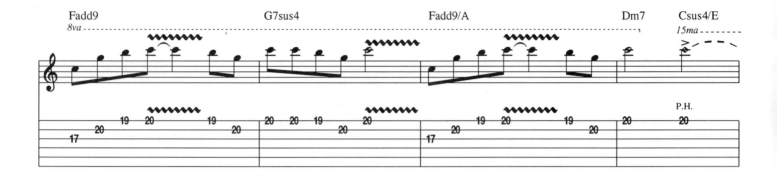

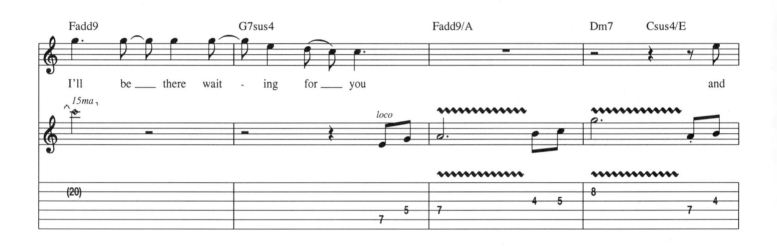

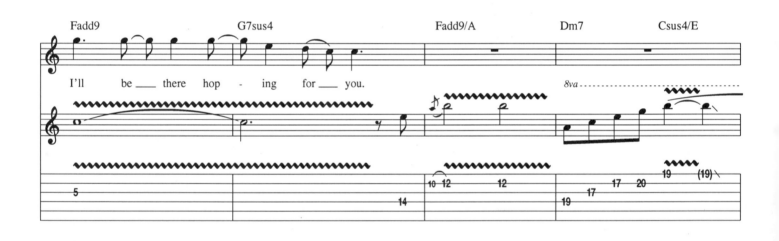

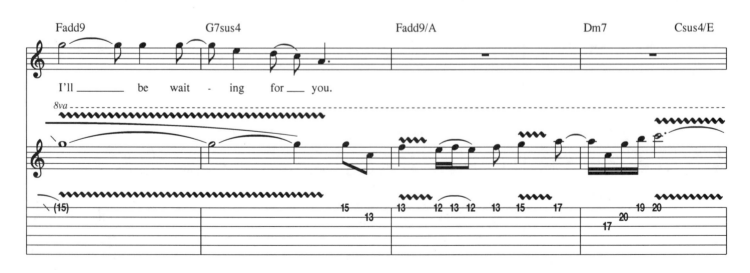

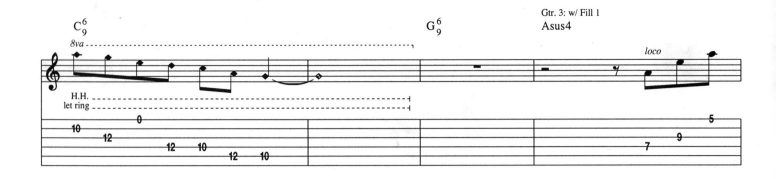

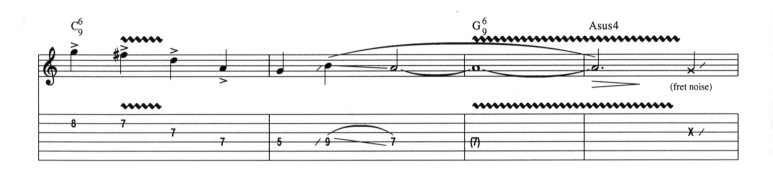

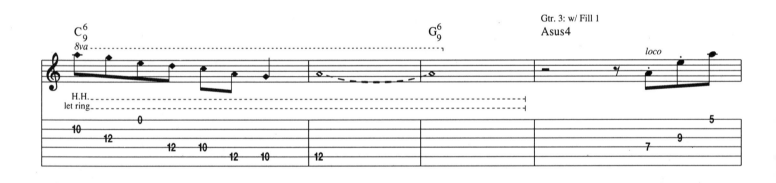

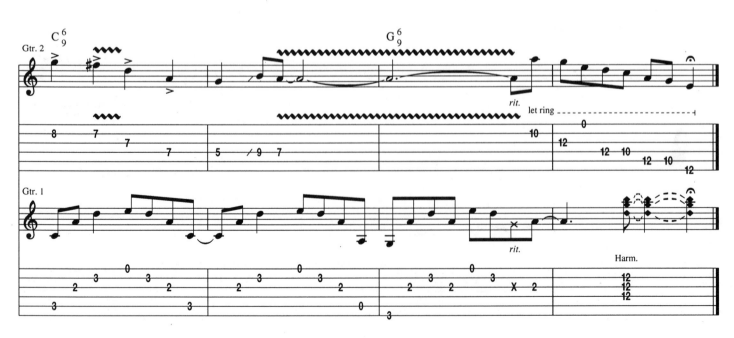

Cliffs Of Dover

By Eric Johnson

24

Desert Rose

Words and Music by Eric Johnson and Vince Mariani

1. Des - ert Rose_ that danc - es in heat of the _ sky. I must pat - tern my life a -
2. Ac - ro - lith _ re - flec - tion that floats through my_ dreams. Ar - id is _ the dust un - der -

bout you. You can make_ the most_ when the _ wa - ters runs dry.
neath me. Some-thing far _ a - way,_ a mir - age so it seems.

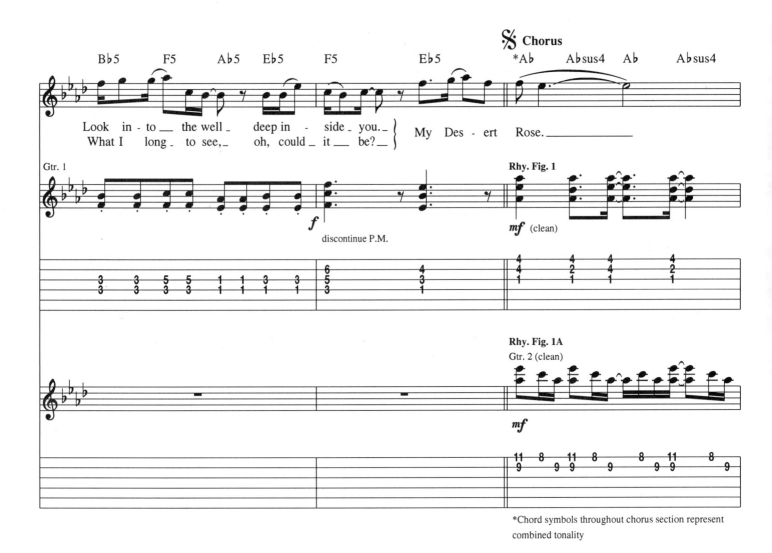

*Chord symbols throughout chorus section represent combined tonality

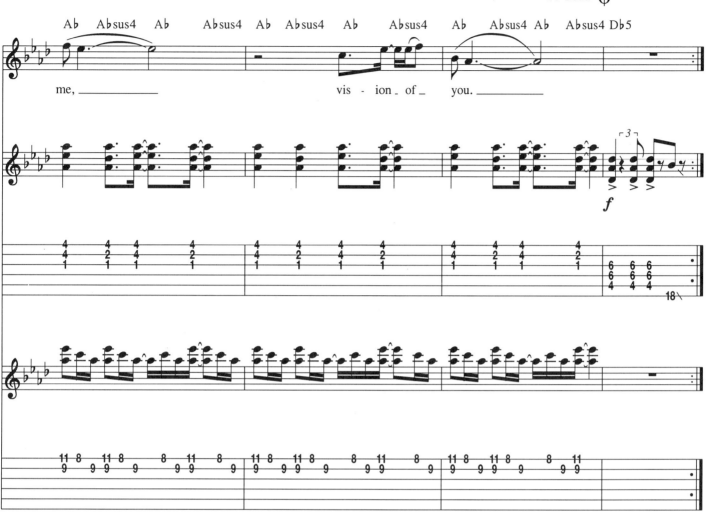

Guitar Solo

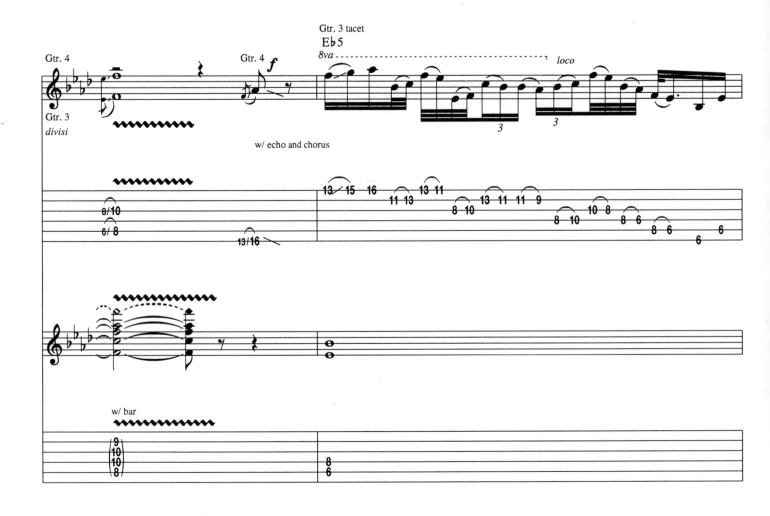

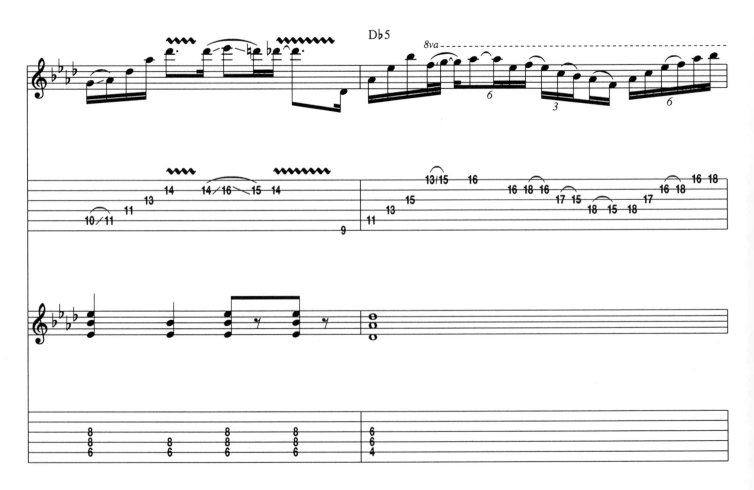

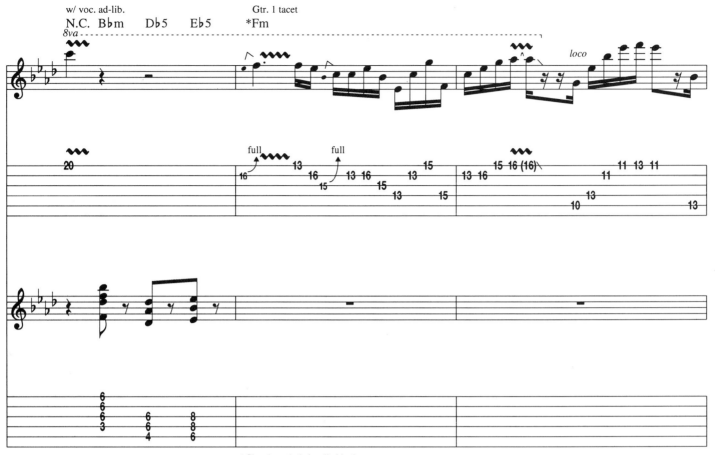

*Chord symbols implied by bass.

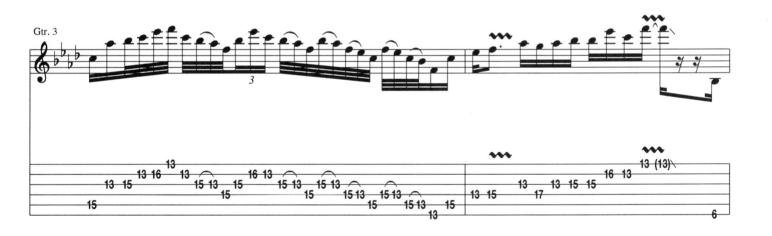

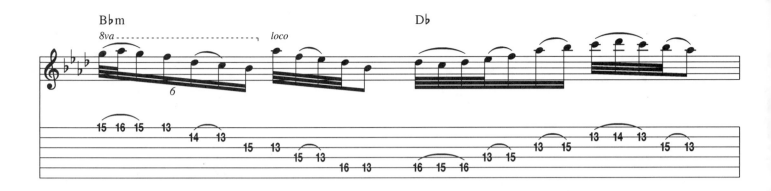

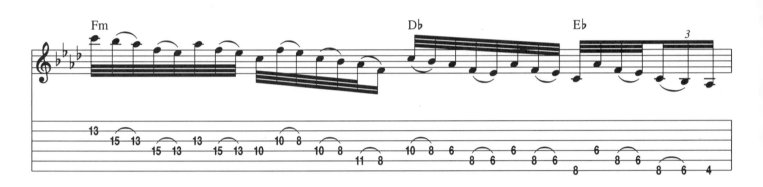

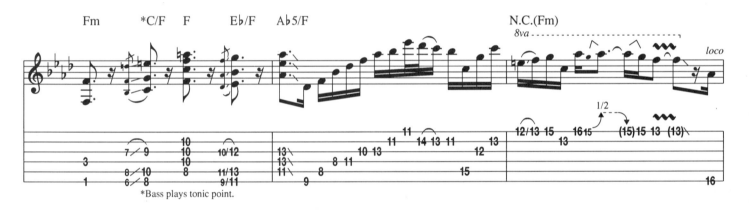

*Bass plays tonic point.

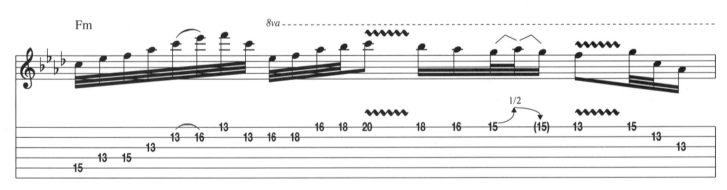

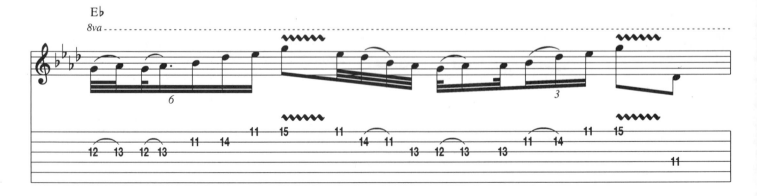

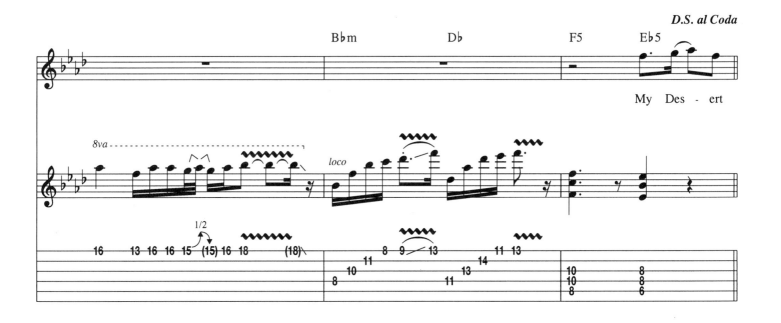

⊕ *Coda*

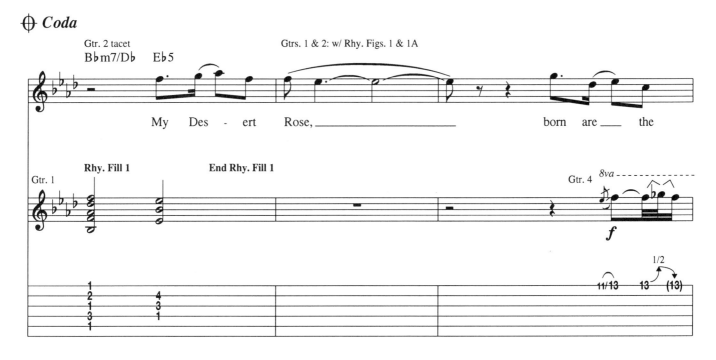

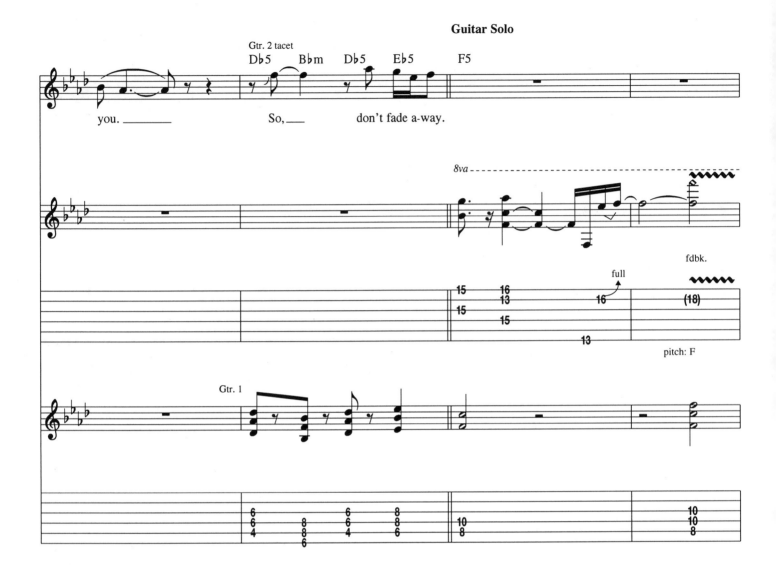

you. _____ So, ___ don't fade a-way.

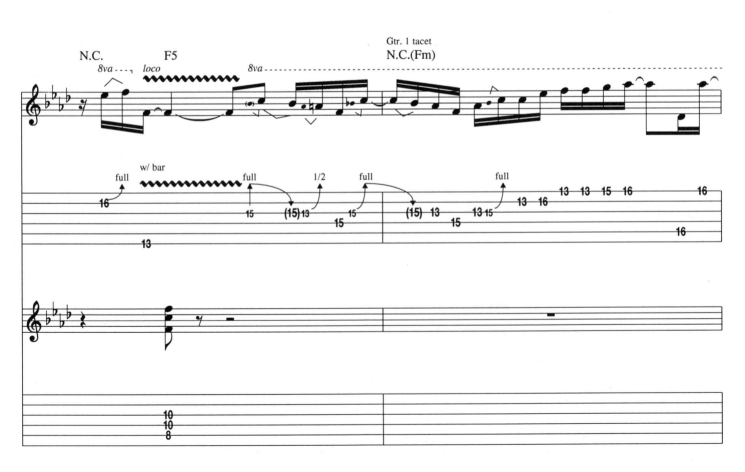

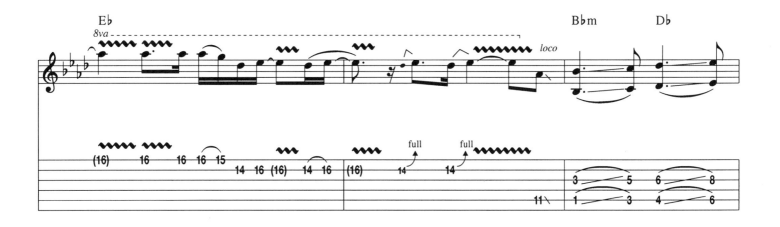

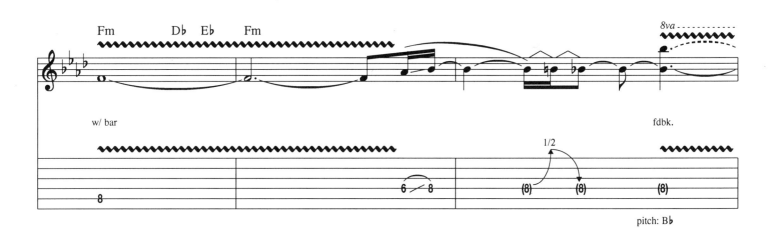

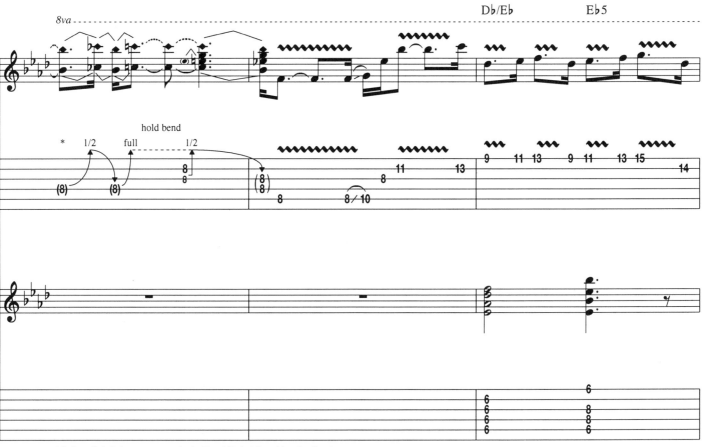

*Strings 2 & 3 ring out sympathetically while holding 4th string bend.

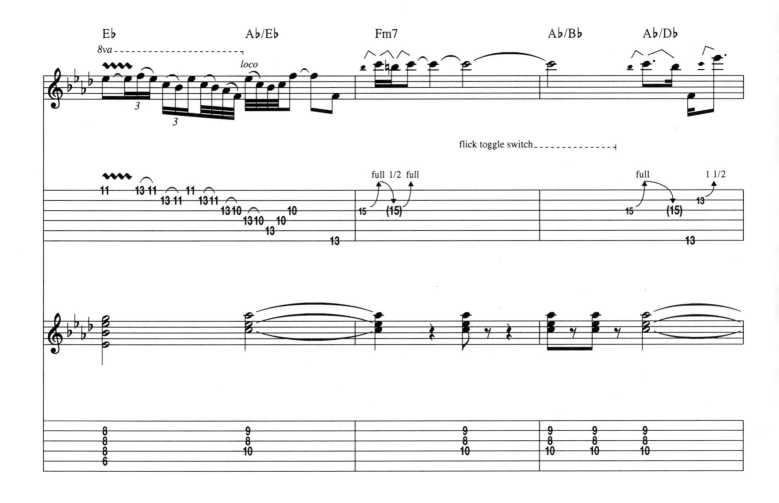

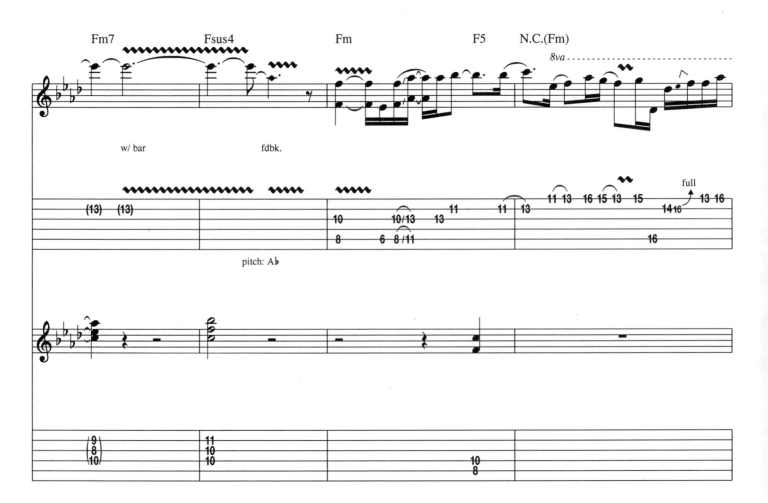

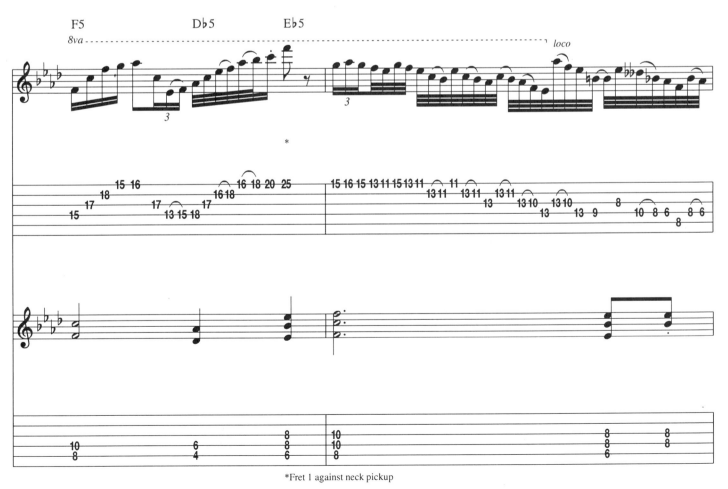

*Fret 1 against neck pickup

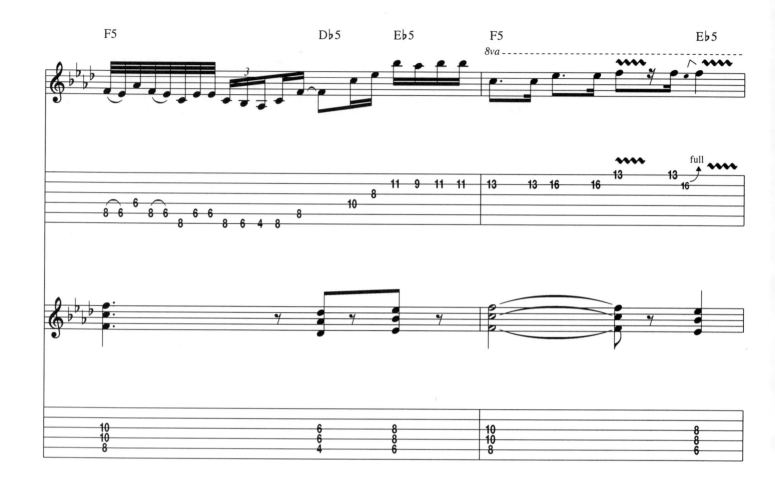

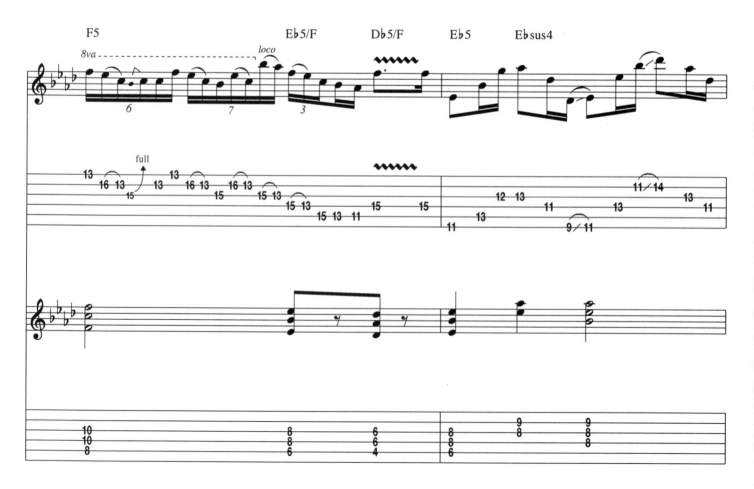

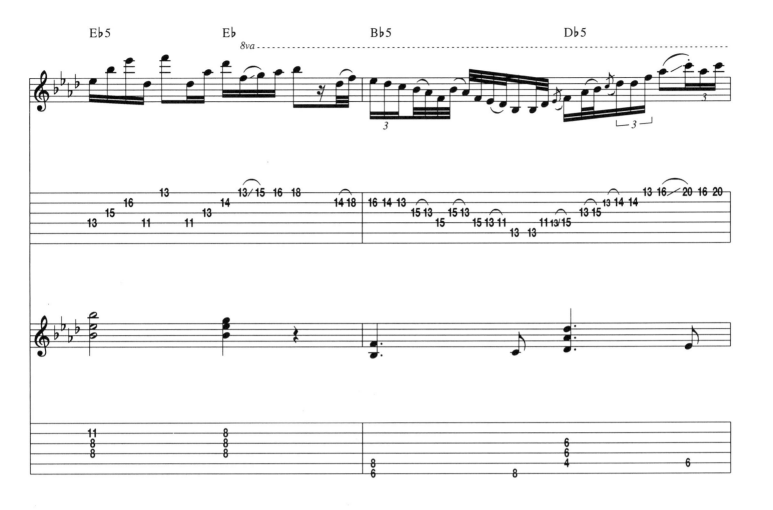

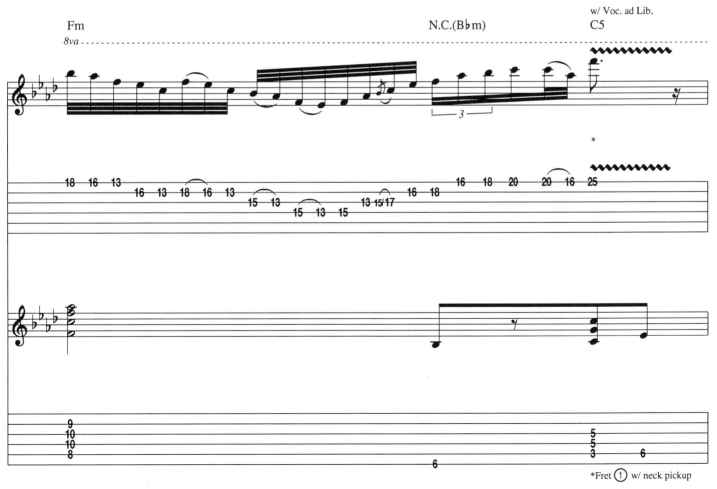

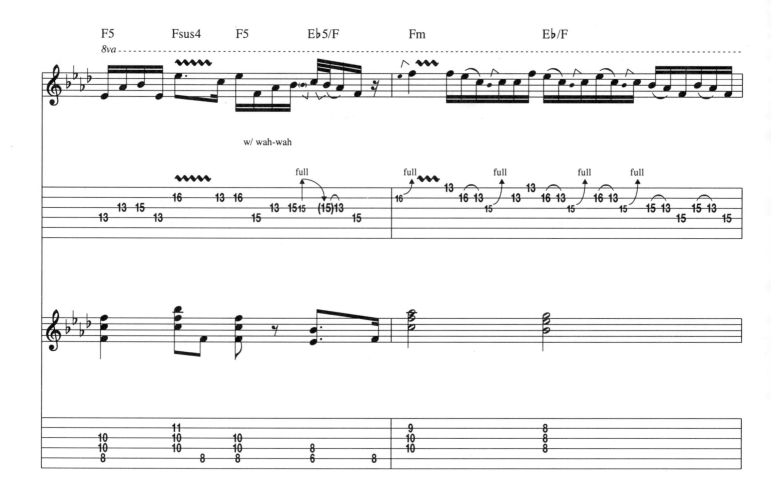

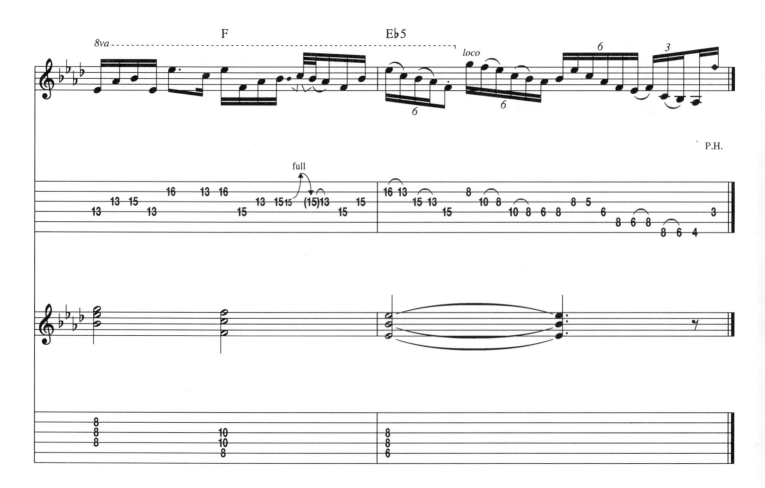

East Wes

By Eric Johnson

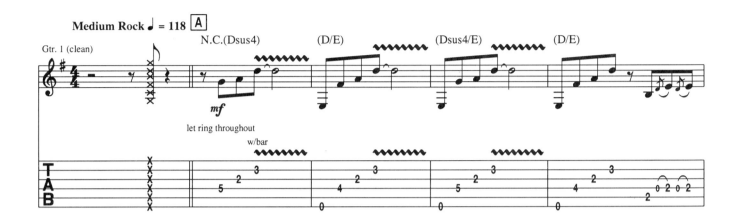

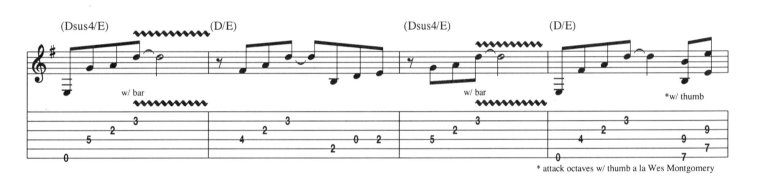

* attack octaves w/ thumb a la Wes Montgomery

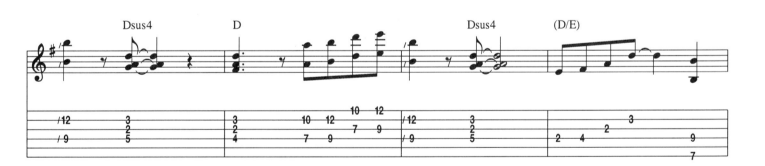

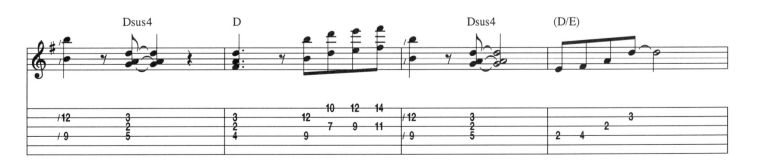

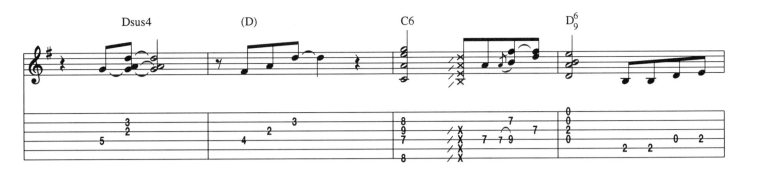

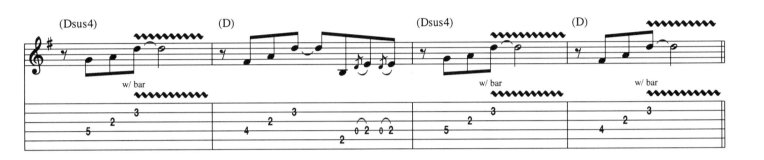

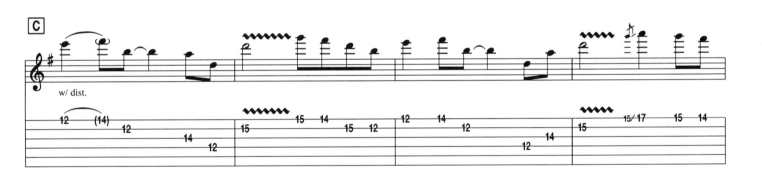

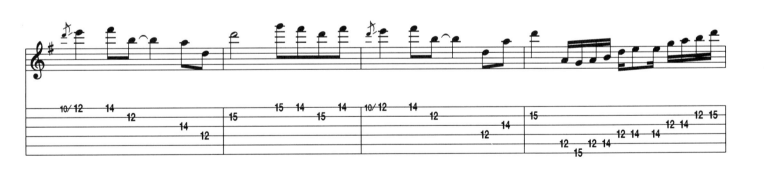

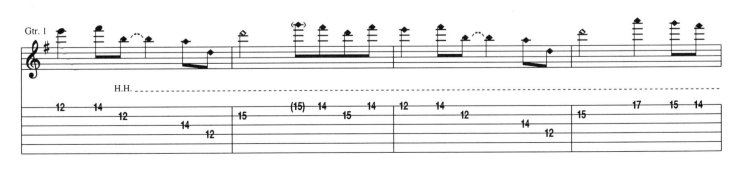

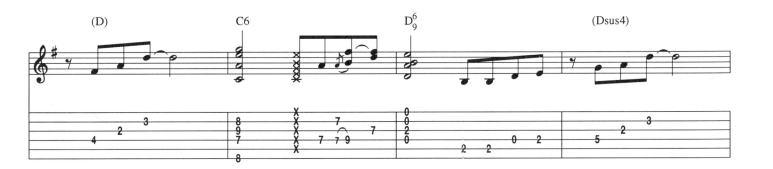

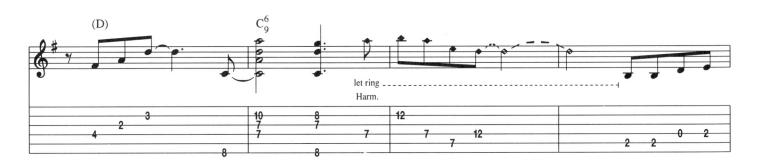

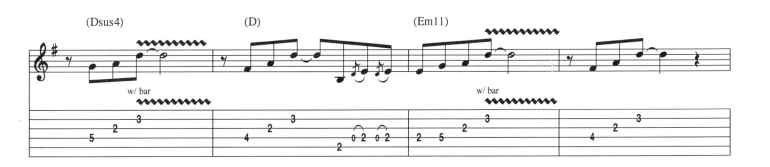

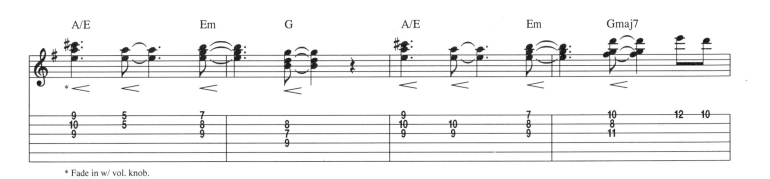

* Fade in w/ vol. knob.

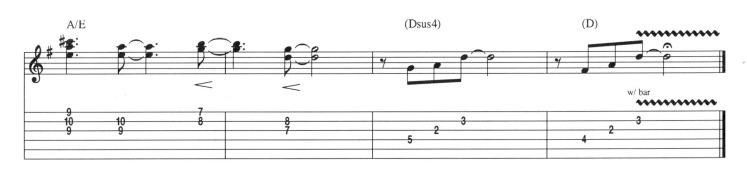

Nothing Can Keep Me From You

By Eric Johnson

NOTE: Bass plays tonic pedal point throughout verse.

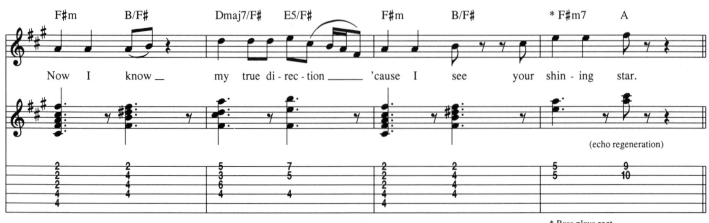

* Bass plays root.

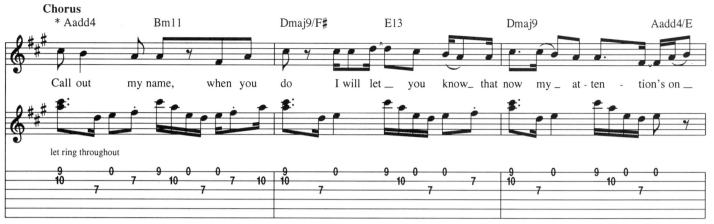

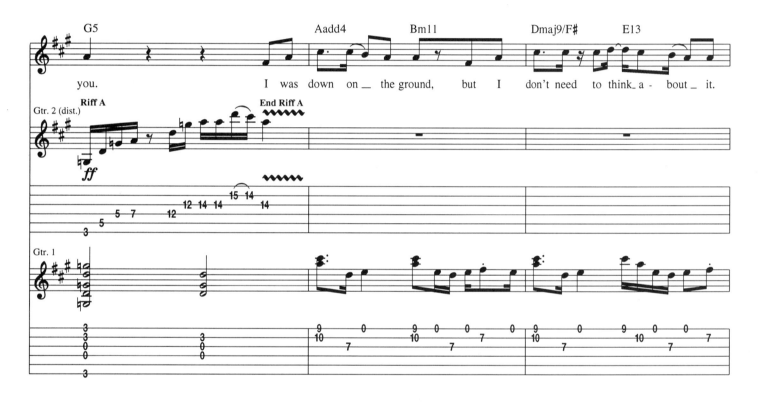

Verse

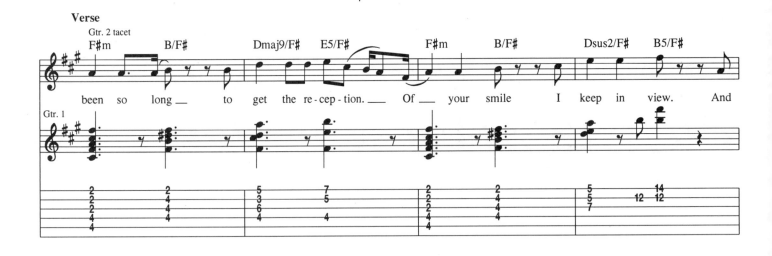

been so long __ to get the re-cep-tion. __ Of __ your smile I keep in view. And

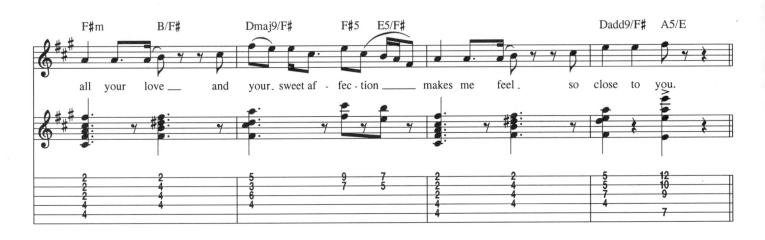

all your love __ and your sweet af - fec - tion __ makes me feel __ so close to you.

% Chorus

Call out my name, when you do I will let _ you know _ that now my _ at - ten - tion's on __

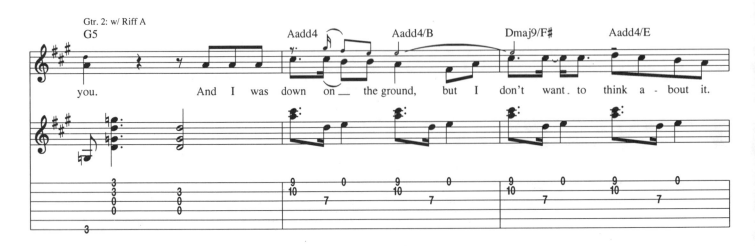

you. And I was down on __ the ground, but I don't want to think a - bout it.

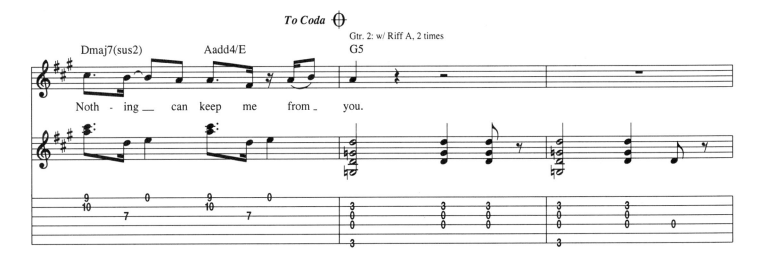

Nothing can keep me from you.

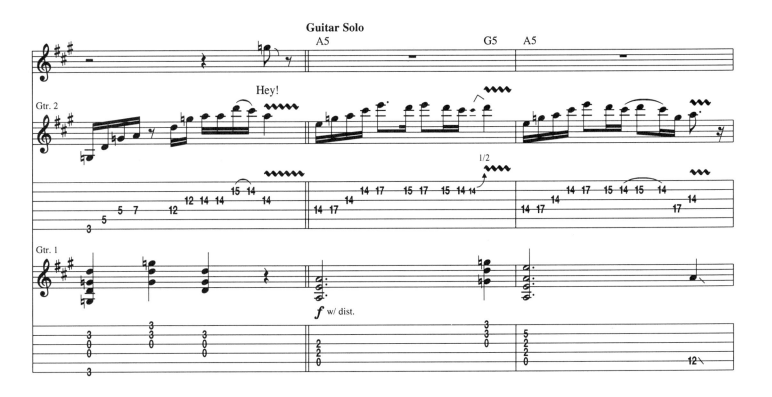

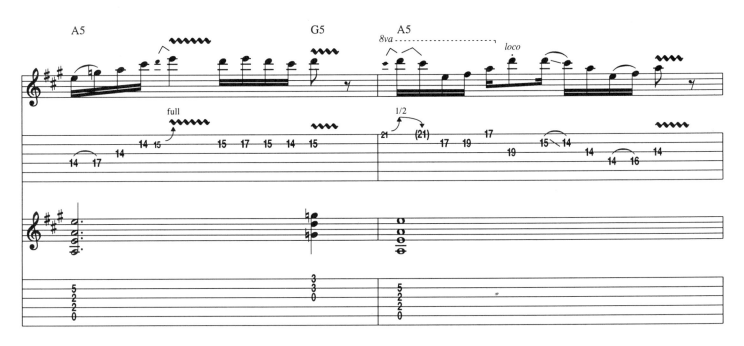

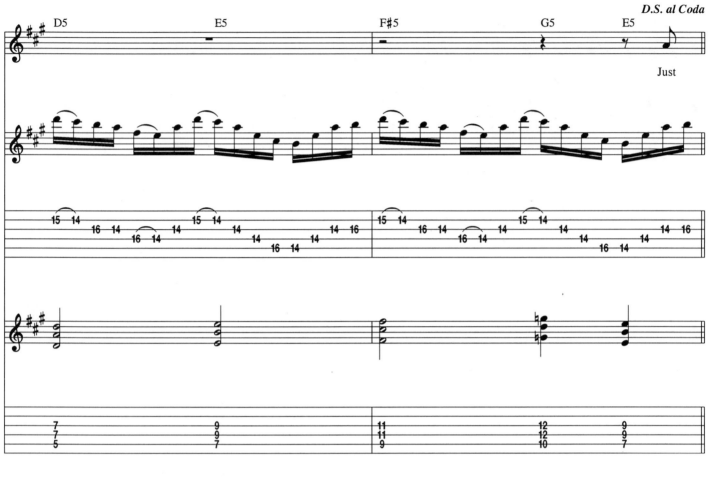

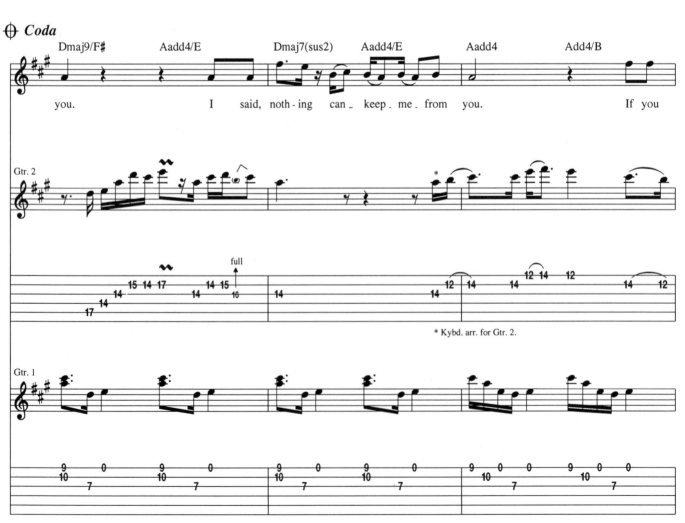

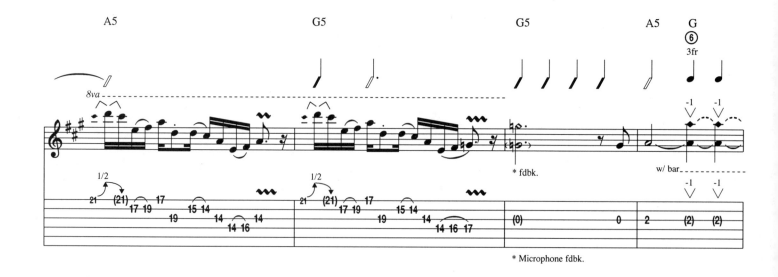

* Microphone fdbk.

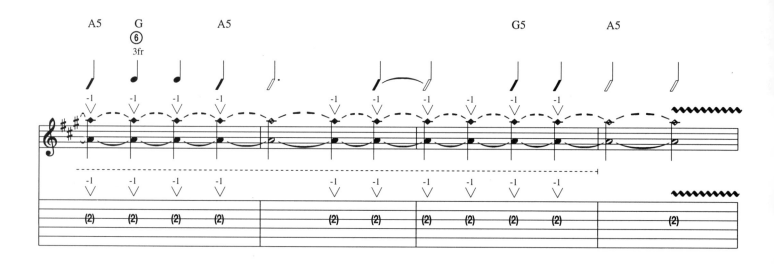

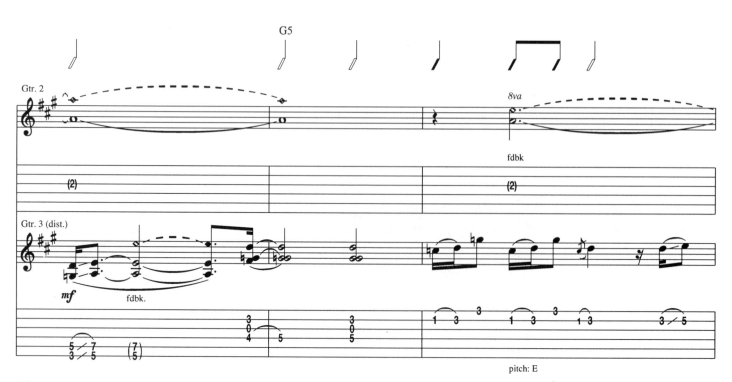

pitch: E

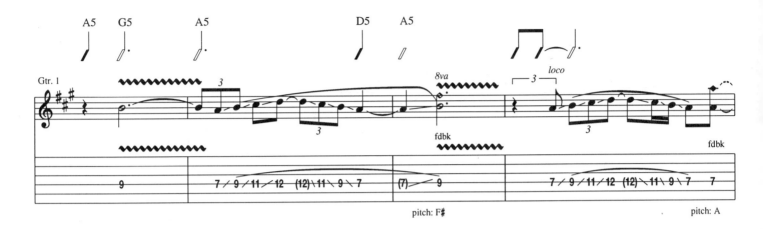

Begin Fade

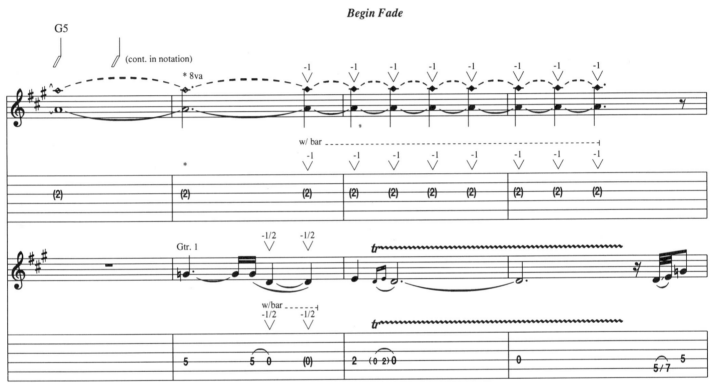

* Fdbk. spontaneously ascends overtone series to next octave.

Fade Out

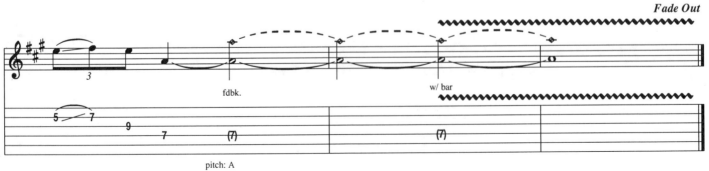

pitch: A

Righteous

By Eric Johnson

Song For George

By Eric Johnson

Drop D Tuning:
① = D ④ = D
② = B ⑤ = A
③ = G ⑥ = D

NOTE: Play finger style throughout w/ thumb plucking bass part (shown with down stems).

Soulful Terrain

By Eric Johnson

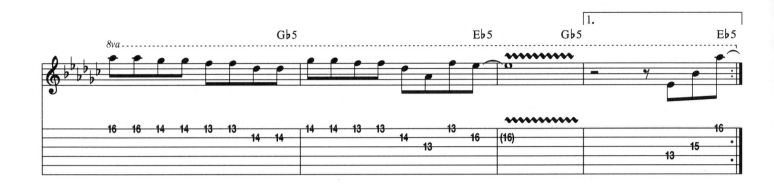

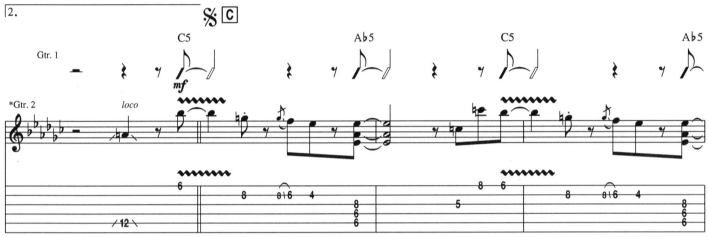

*with added gain

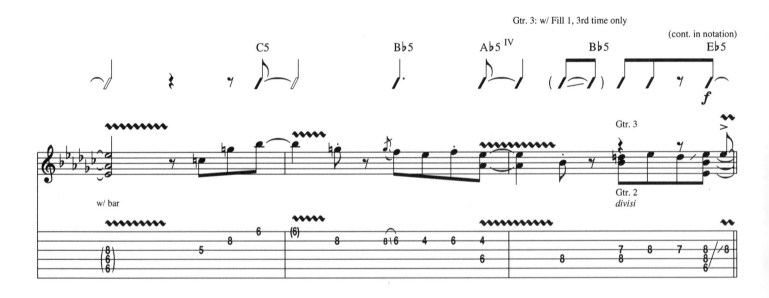

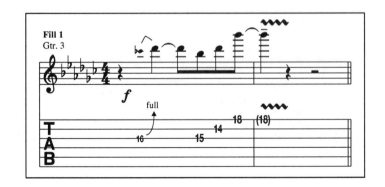

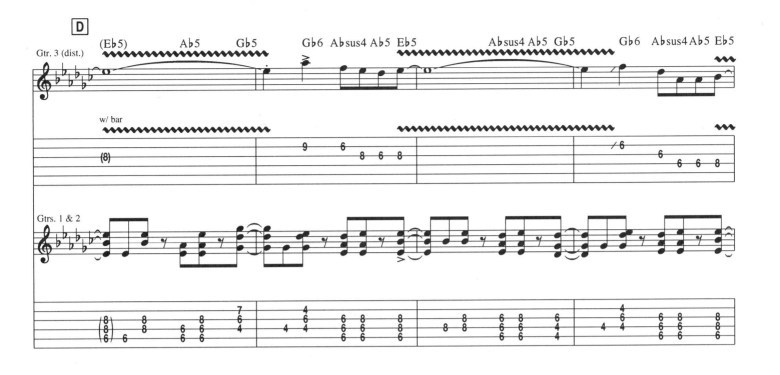

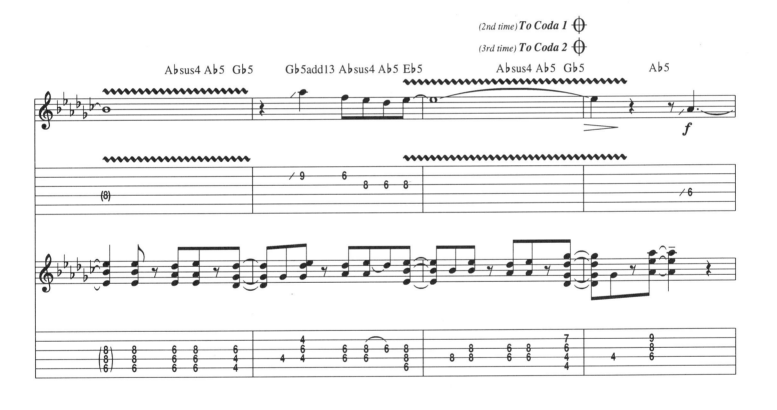

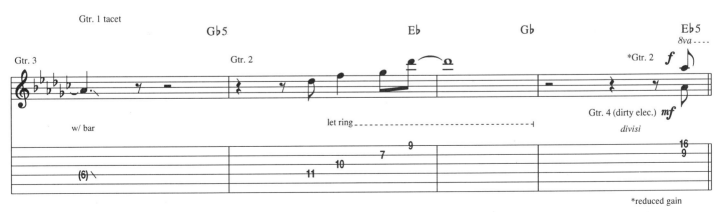

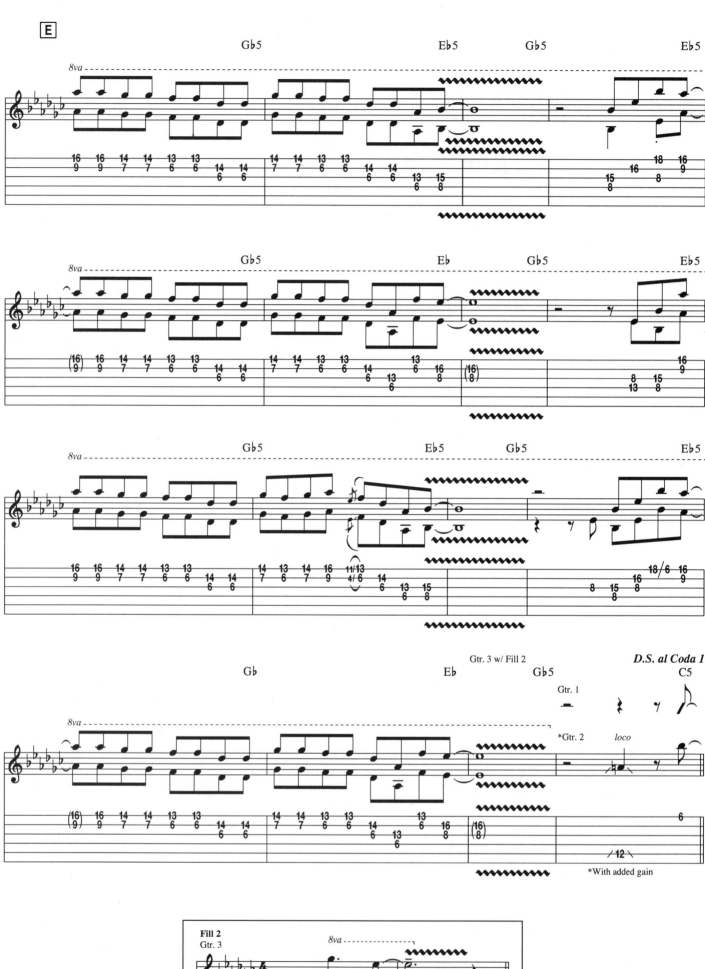

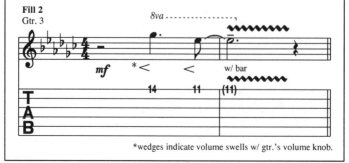

*wedges indicate volume swells w/ gtr.'s volume knob.

Coda 1

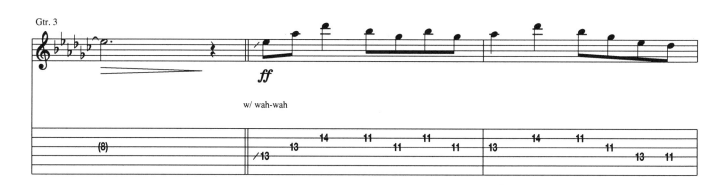

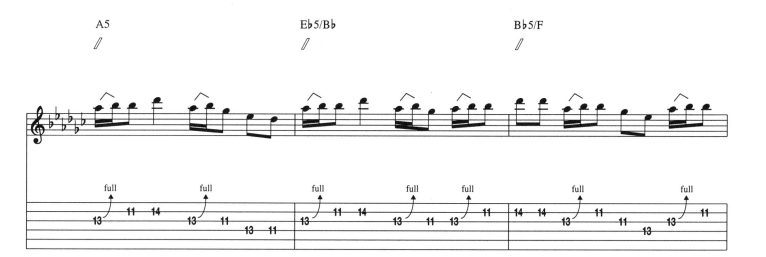

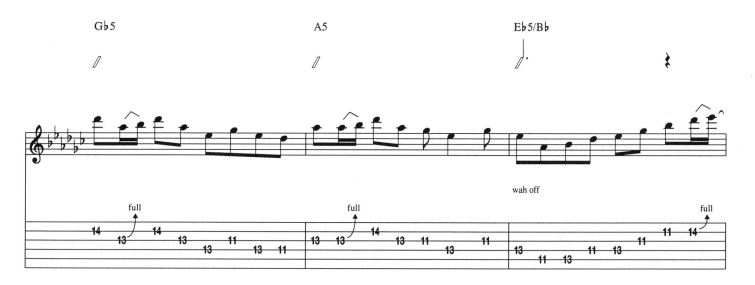

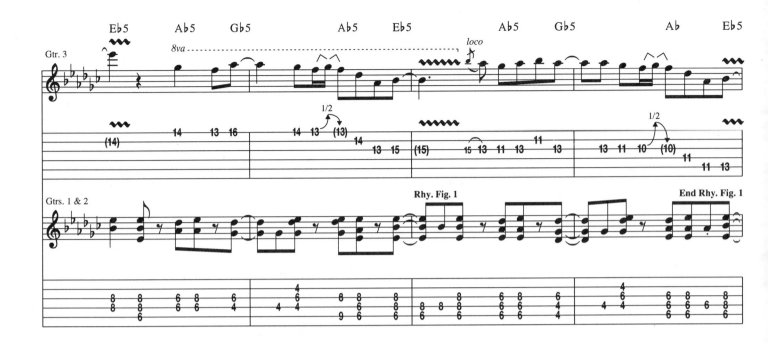

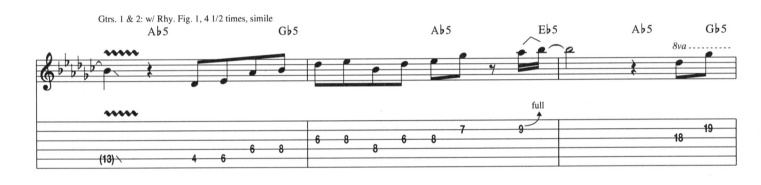

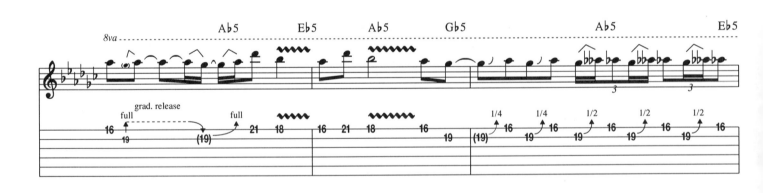

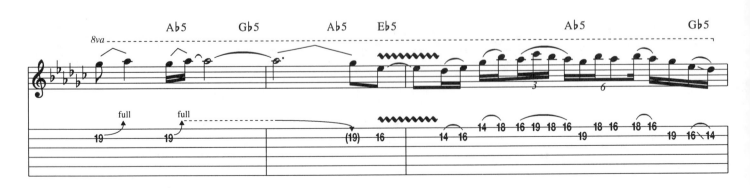

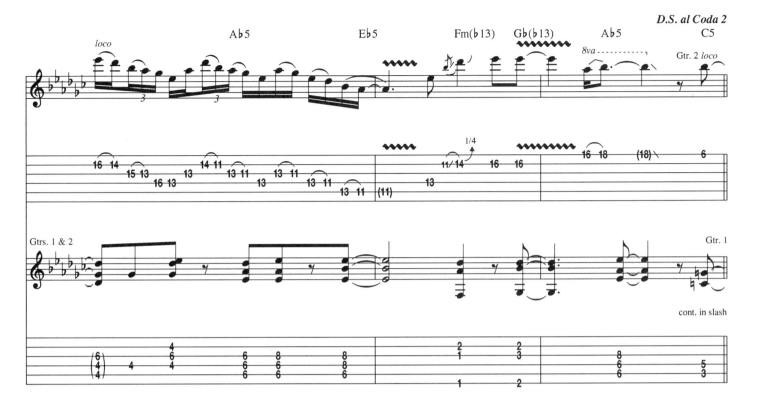

Coda 2

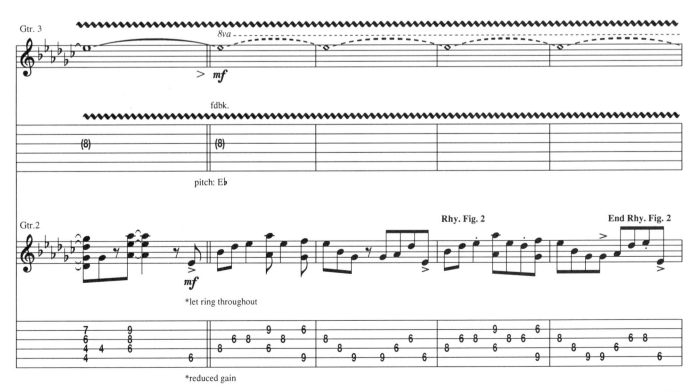

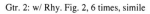

Gtr. 2: w/ Rhy. Fig. 2, 6 times, simile

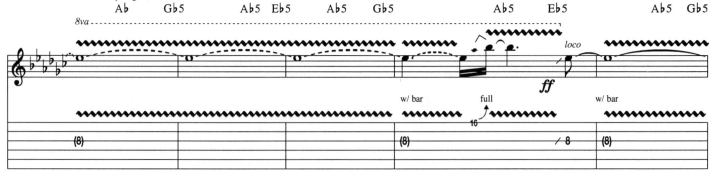

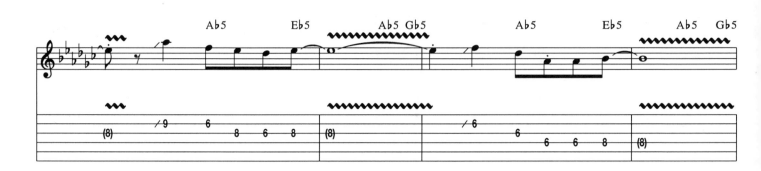

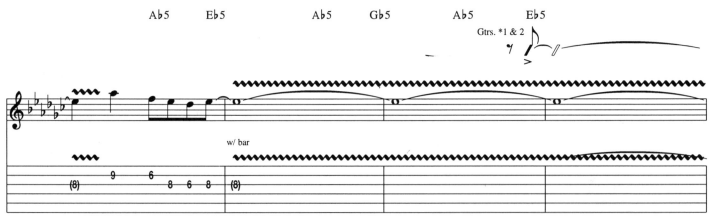

*Gtr. 1 at **ff** dynamic level w/ added gain.

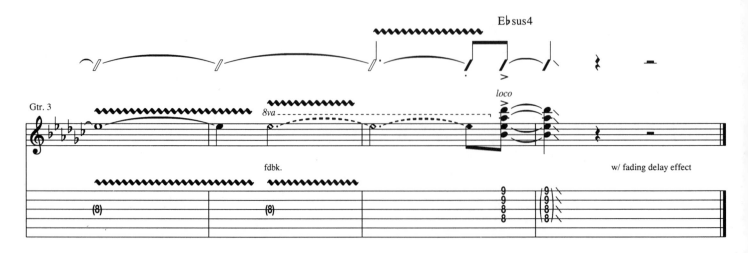

Steve's Boogie

By Eric Johnson

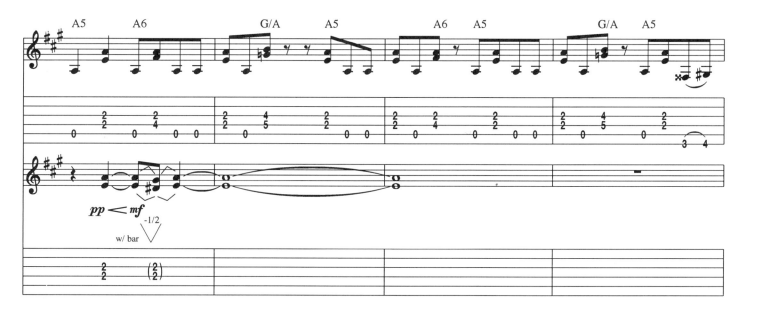

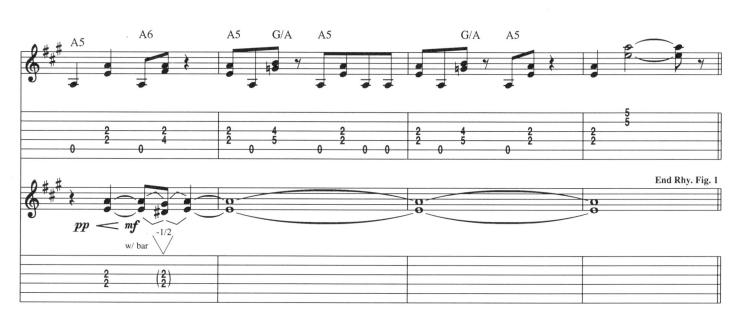

C Guitar Solo

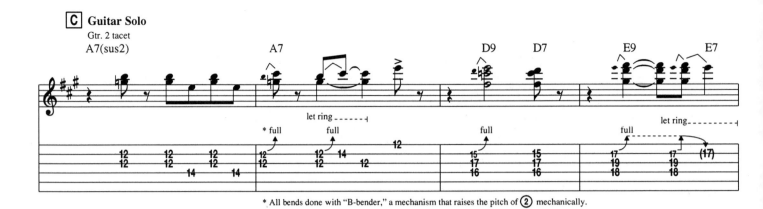

* All bends done with "B-bender," a mechanism that raises the pitch of ② mechanically.

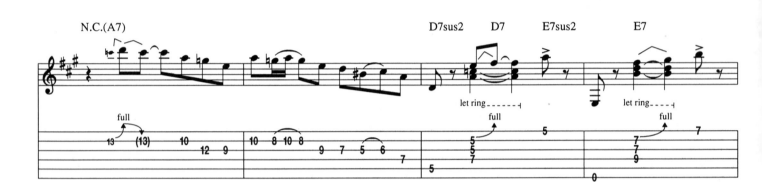

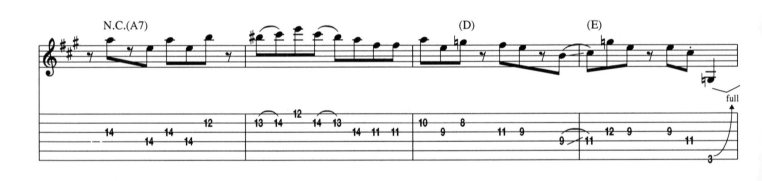

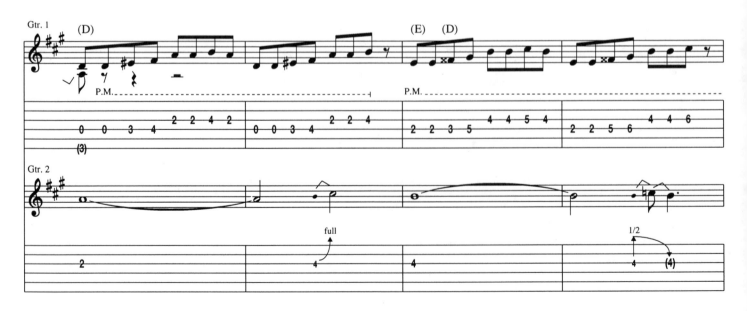

* Ghost bend with "B bender."

Gtr. 2 tacet

A5

Gtrs. 1 & 2

Trademark

By Eric Johnson

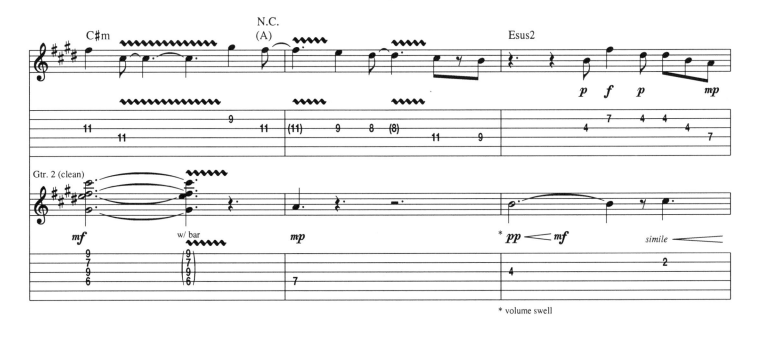

* volume swell

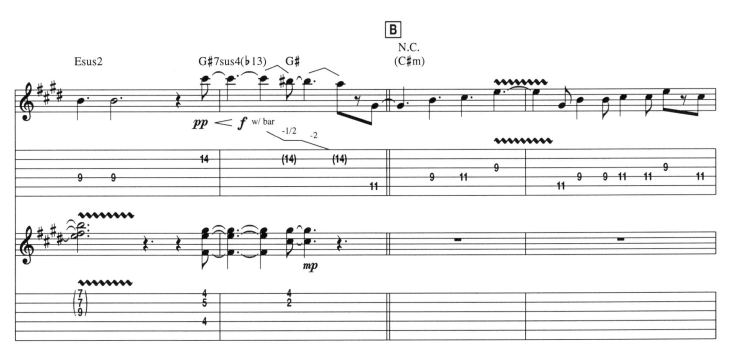

Note: Guitar plays partial chords. Overall harmony implied by bass.
* no third

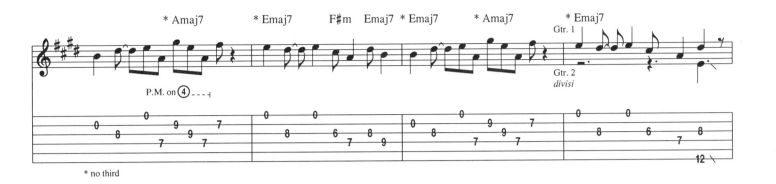

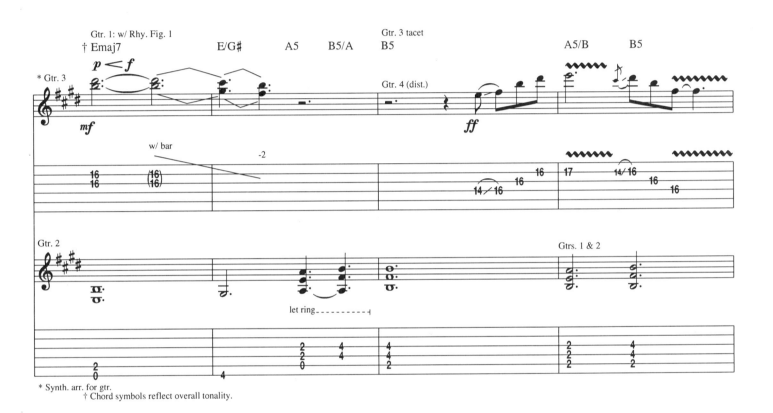

* Synth. arr. for gtr.
  † Chord symbols reflect overall tonality.

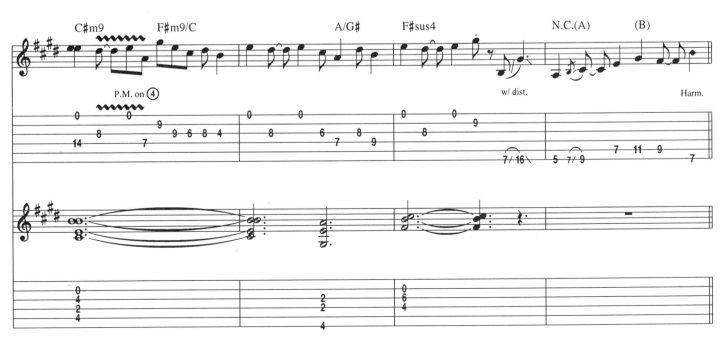

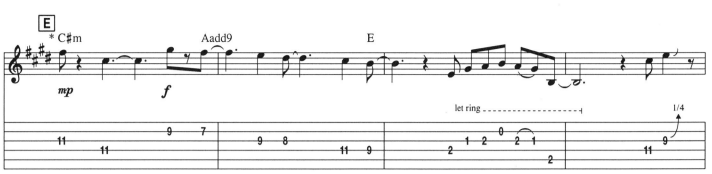

* Chords implied by kybd.

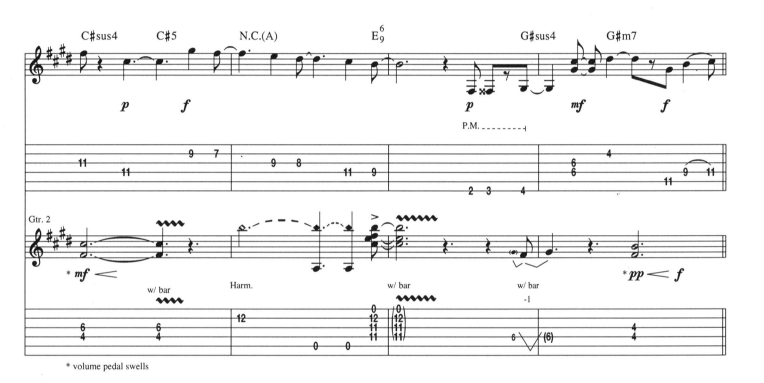

* volume pedal swells

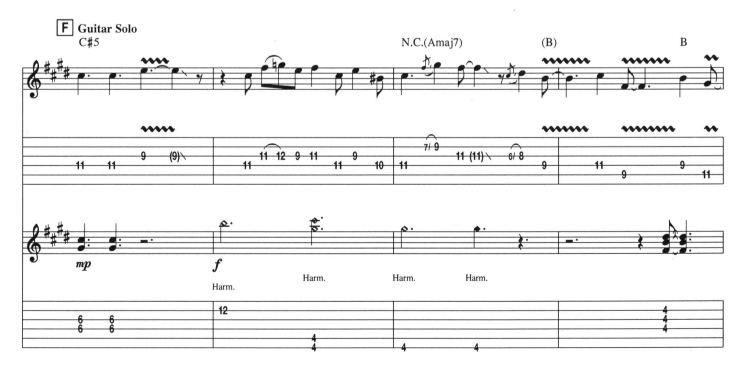

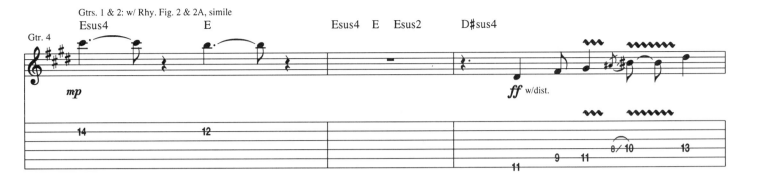

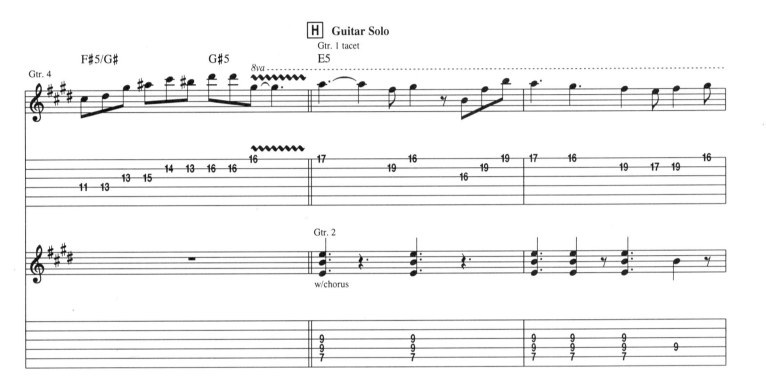

* Bass plays E.

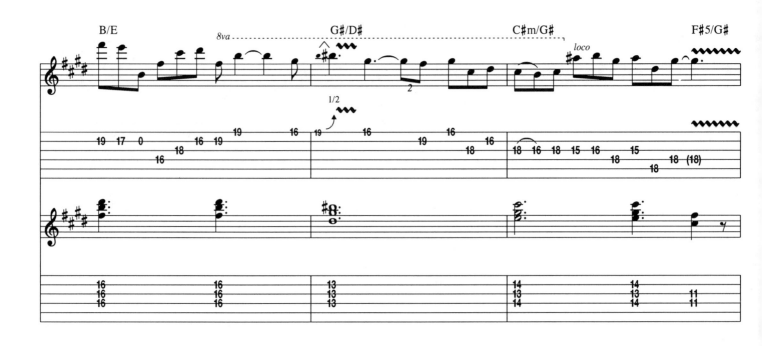

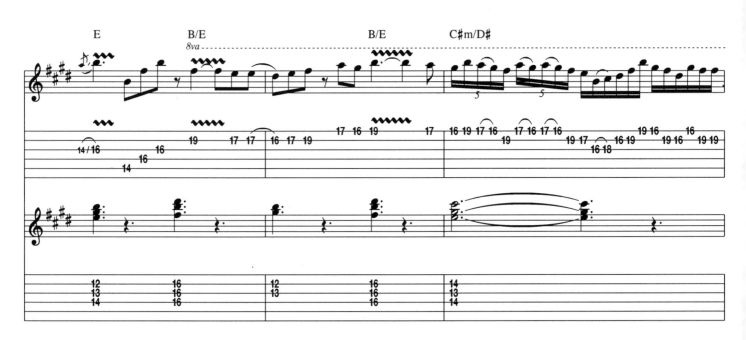

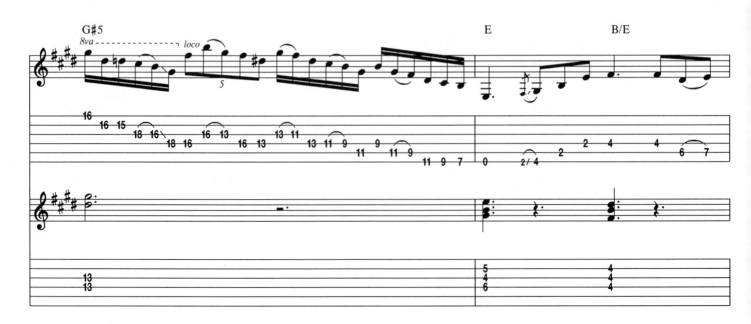

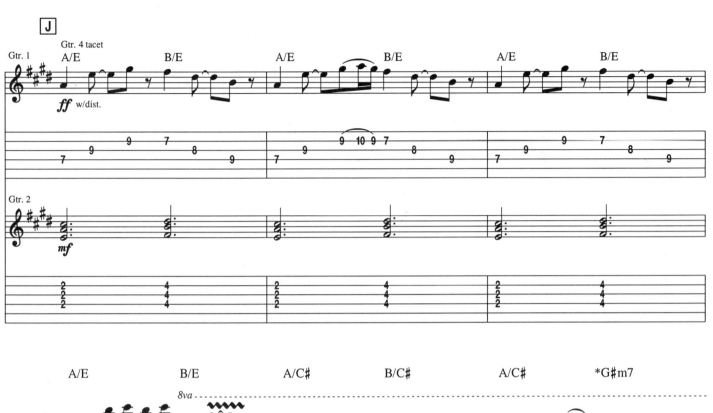

* Bass plays G#.

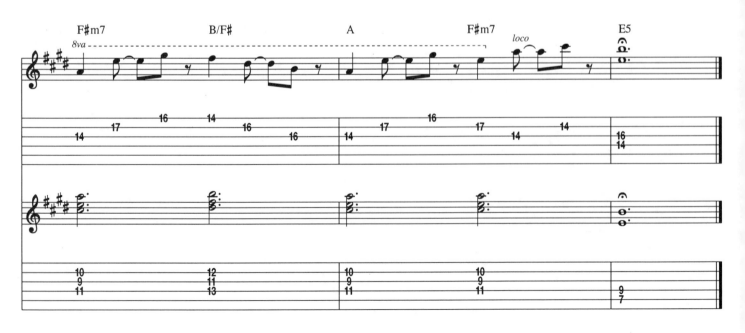

Victory

By Eric Johnson, Roscoe Beck and Tommy Taylor

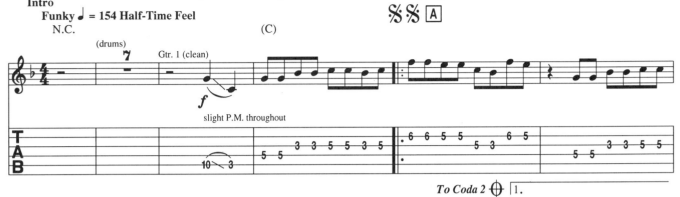

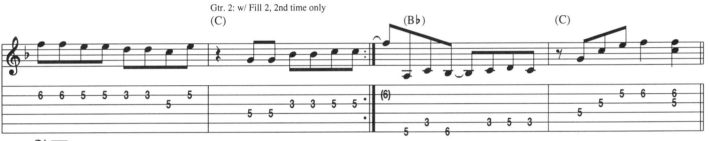

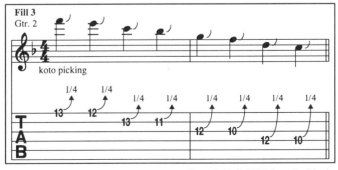

⊕ *Coda 1*

Zap

By Eric Johnson

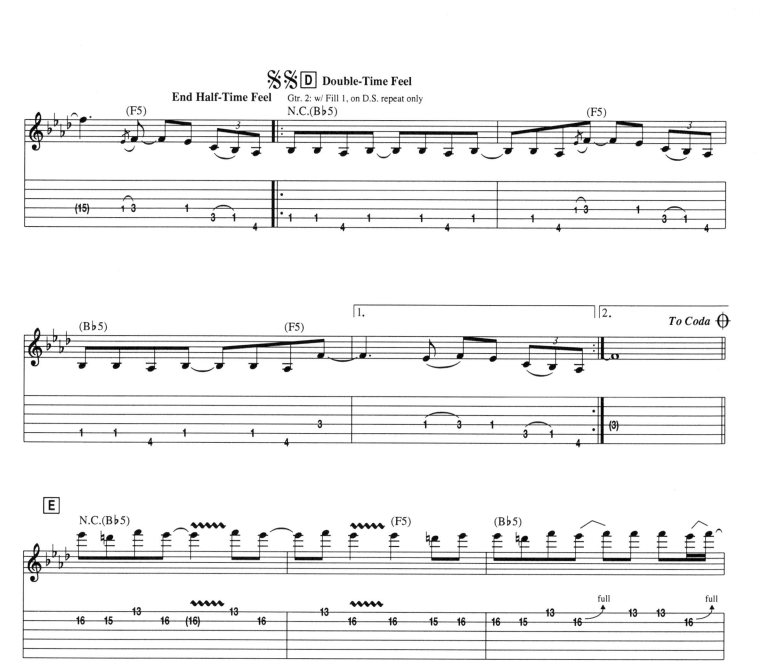

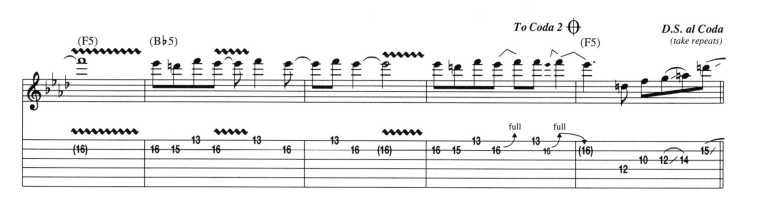

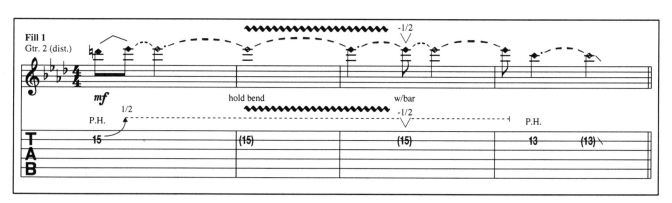

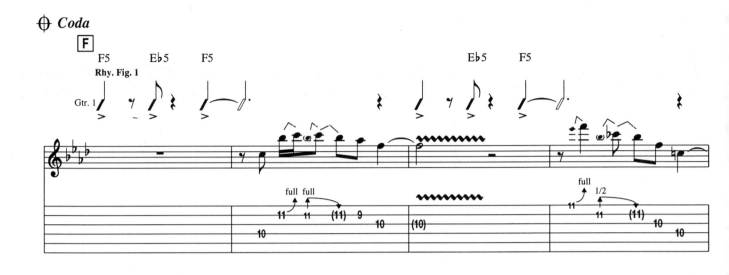

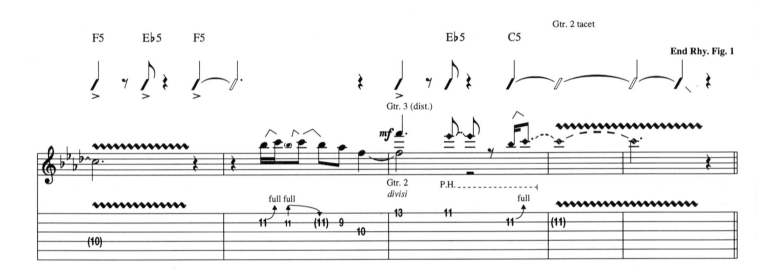

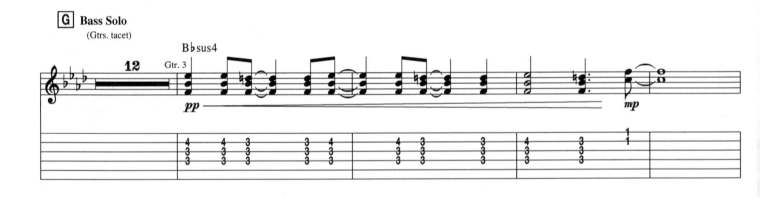

* Played ahead of the beat.

NOTATION LEGEND